The Nose Knows

by Patricia Ann Lynch
illustrations by Alex De Lange

Harcourt Brace & Company

Orlando   Atlanta   Austin   Boston   San Francisco   Chicago   Dallas   New York   Toronto   London

Joan knows a lot. "Call me The Nose," Joan says. "No job is too big. The Nose knows!" So on most days, children spoke to Joan. They spoke on the phone. They spoke at Joan's home.

Joan put on an old coat and a big nose. Joan showed Josh how to tell jokes.

Joan wrote a note in code
for Bob. Joan found Rose's
gold yo-yo and Jo's lost frog.

One day Tom rode to Joan's home. "My mom wrote this note," he told Joan. "I was going to shop, but the note ripped."

"Show me the note," Joan told Tom. Both Tom and Joan looked at the note. Most of the note was not there!

Tom moaned, "I don't know what Mom wrote."

"Don't moan. Don't groan," Joan told Tom. "This is a job for The Nose!"

"Dog boats?" said Joan. "No. Dog bows? No. Dog boxes? I don't think so."

Then Joan said, "The Nose knows! It's dog bones!" She wrote DOG BONES on the note.

"Hot rope?" said Joan. "No. Hot roses? No. Hot rocks? I don't think so." Then Joan said, "The Nose knows! It's hot rolls!" She wrote HOT ROLLS on the note.

"Cold coffee?" said Joan.
"No. Cold coal? No. Cold
coconuts? I don't think so."

Then Joan said, "The Nose
knows! It's cold cola!" She
wrote COLD COLA on the note.
"Thanks, Joan!" Tom said.

Now Tom could shop. He
got what was on the note.
Then Tom went home.

"Good job, Tom!" his
mom said.